**Once...** *A Journey Through Life* is my first book. The story is based on a journey through a surreal world of emotions. It is a lifetime of emotions in words and pictures from my imagination to yours. I hope that you enjoy the story and the art, and feel free to comment. I *love* feedback.

www.pattyhallart.com

pattyhallart@gmail.com

# Introduction

**I've always been a visual person.** Someone will say something in conversation or something will catch my eye, and next thing you know, I'm scrambling for paper and pencil. It's a race to scribble down whatever has popped into my head, so I don't lose the image or the phrase that strikes me at that moment. You will see some of these images in the pages of this book.

The poem within this book was started many years ago with some of my little scribbles. I pieced a couple of phrases together, and the story just started. But I didn't know how to end it, so it was set aside, and of course, it was forgotten. Eventually, I dug it up again and worked on it some more, but I still had no ending for it. Oh yeah! - I set it aside again.

By this time, the images started to creep into my brain and onto paper. Well, after many years I found the poem once again. A little more work, and there was my ending. Finally, the words to bring my story to a close! Well, at that point, I just had to combine the whole thing into one final, finished piece. *Please enjoy*.

This book is dedicated to;
my children & my grandchildren

<u>With All My Love</u>

For
Amy & Mike,
Briana, Ellise, Gianni,
Natalie, & Mykayla

# Once...

upon a *magical* time...

In a mystical, far-away land,

Where dreams are plucked from beautiful trees,
    and teddy bears sleep in the sand;

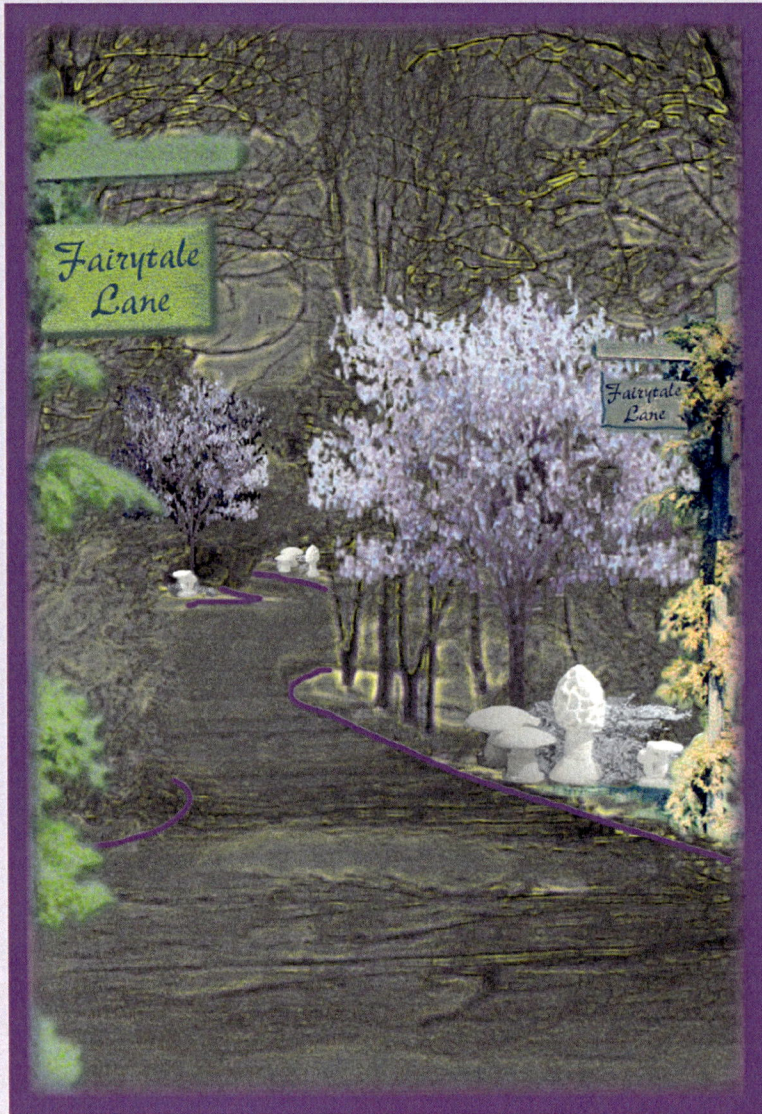

... I was walking down Fairytale Lane ...

There, I met
a strange man
named Chagrin.

"Won't you walk with me
down to the Sea of Surprise?"

He asked, with a mystical grin.

So we walked through the Lullaby Forest
Where the trees sing their songs to the air,

and over the Mountains of

Faith, Hope, and Love,

(We walked past
the Road of Despair).

Then we walked through the

*Fields of Fantasy*

Where the flowers bloom...

...all the year round.

Where fairies and elves play their games of delight
...when the morning dew lifts from the ground.

Finally we came to the

*Sea of Surprise!*

and there in the fading daylight
stood the most beautiful ship
that I ever saw.

It was radiant — it          with light.

1

Well we boarded the ship and sailed away
To the Land of Goodness and Joy.
There, we anchored our boat
in the Harbor of Wealth,

# ... At the Dock of the Times You Enjoy.

We had sailed all night and into the dawn
Telling folktales and learning the lore
Of the friendly and innocent natives
That would be there lining the shore.

The sparkling blue sun...

        sprayed a rainbow of gold

Through the feathery cobwebs of clouds.

And the love in the air melted over the land,

Like a blanket of snow on the ground.

Harmony, a quiet town,
rested safely by the sea.
The natives were timid and cautious,
yet filled with Eager
Curiosity.

They lived in peaceful comfort...
and with great Appreciation.
Their lives had Clarity and Balance.
They had high hopes...
and asperations.

These were kind and friendly people,
and we wished that we could stay.
But our journey was not yet over,

so we went upon our way.

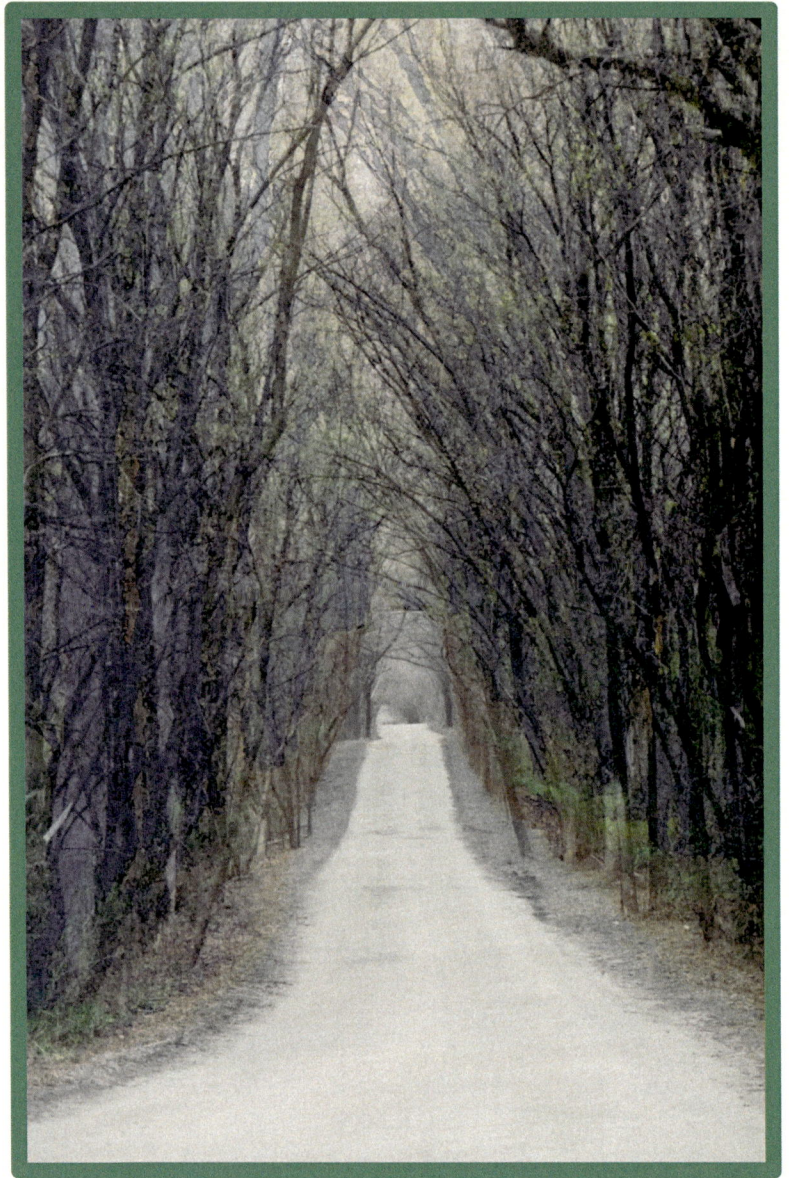

We traveled along

Responsible Road

With a bit of hesitation…

and we climbed the Hills of Hardship
...with steady Determination.

The prosperous city of Justice
sat upon the Mountain high.
Majestic to behold —

golden spires to the sky.

The townsfolk were blessed with Abundance
They were playful and graciously **Bold**.
Their lives were consumed with perfection,
yet their demeanor seemed distant... and cold.

We stayed in town just long enough to gather our supplies,

... and we camped on the outskirts of town that night –

under vast and starlit skies.

The birds sang their
love songs
of passion.

While the animals
danced with delight.

They sang and they danced...
they laughed and they ate

...Til the moon shed its beautiful light.

There was a journey ahead
in the morning,
so we camped under twinkling stars.

All through the night —
we listened in dreams,
to soft mumblings
from flutes and guitars.

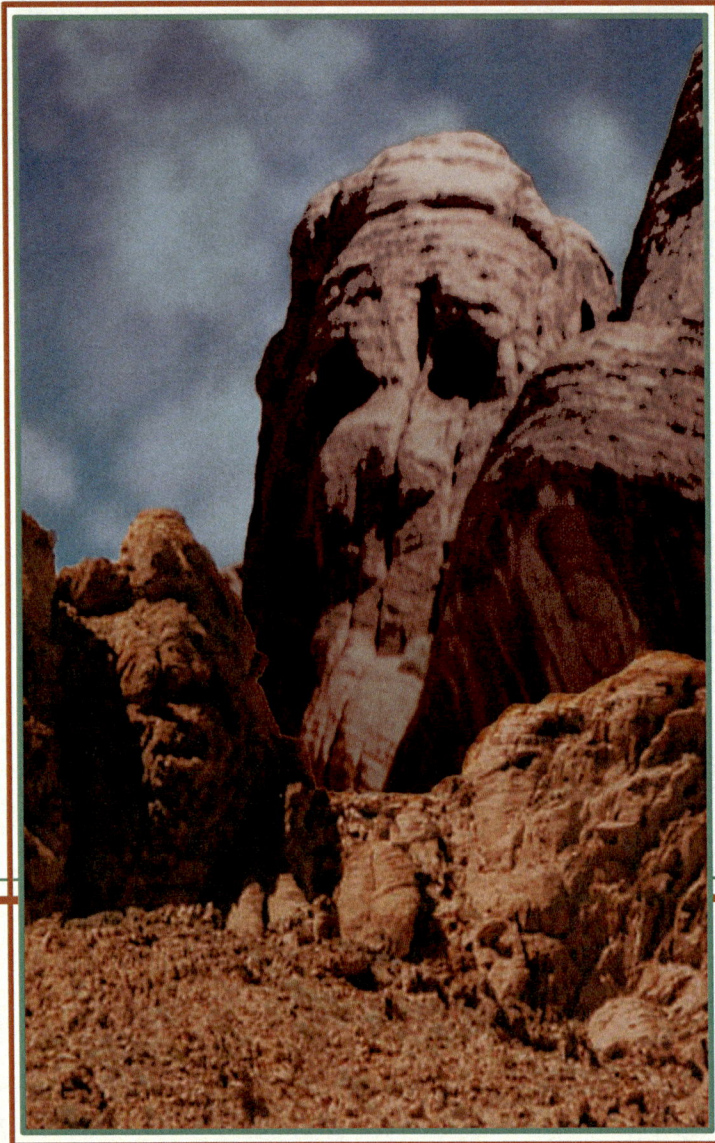

In the morning we woke
with the sunrise
And started our trek
'cross the land.

When we
finally reached the
Rock of Regret...

Sadly,

Chagrin took my hand...

"There's something amiss in this country.

I feel mayhem and rage in the air.

'Tis certain this land is in danger!

We must let the world know that we care!"

Then we ventured out into the mist

Of Tales That Have Been Left Untold.

It was dark —

It was damp, —

and the mist gave way...

to the Market of Dreams Bought and Sold.

There were peddlers
and pushers abounding.
There were sad,
sunken faces galore.

It was strange,
it was frightening
and fearsome.

There were secrets behind each locked door!

We didn't bargain for dreams –
but hastened straight through,
Without pausing
or stopping to stare.

We didn't turn our heads…
we kept to our path.

Didn't speak   –
Barely breathed   –

# Didn't dare!

When we came to the Fields of Freedom
We found something terribly wrong.
The flowers were dead...
                    and the birds in the trees
Had stopped singing their light-hearted song.

There were buzzards and scavengers dancing.

They were feeding on waste and decay.

The dance was the Dance of Depression.

The song was the Song of Dismay.

The question that hung on my breath –
"What will bring life to this land?"
I muttered, "Everything's hopeless!"

Once again, Chagrin took my hand.

"Take heart, my friend — Have Faith!
We can right this wrong with love!"

"We'll call on the Winds of Wonderment
That rain from the heavens above."

So he raised up  his arms, and looked to the sky.

Then he called on the wind and the rain
...With a vengeance so fierce,
the earth seemed to shake –

And the land and the seas shared his pain.

The winds whistled in from the mountains...
And the heavens burst forth and cried.
The skies opened up –
and unleashed all their anger...

as the ground beneath our feet heaved and sighed.

I looked to my friend's strength and wisdom,

and the honor that nurtured each limb.

There was honesty in his emotions...

And the land and the seas joined his hymn.

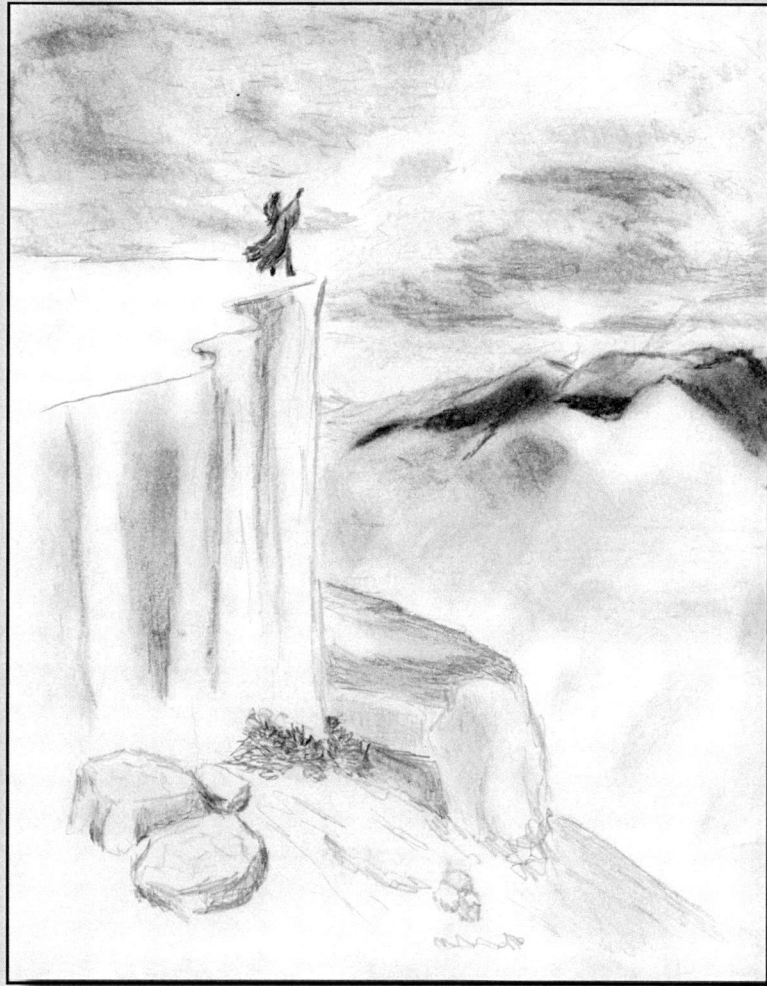

Chagrin
stood alone
in the tempest.

His being
was ravaged and tossed.
He was the land...and the land became him...
He reigned over all that was lost!

We gathered the seeds of Simplicity...

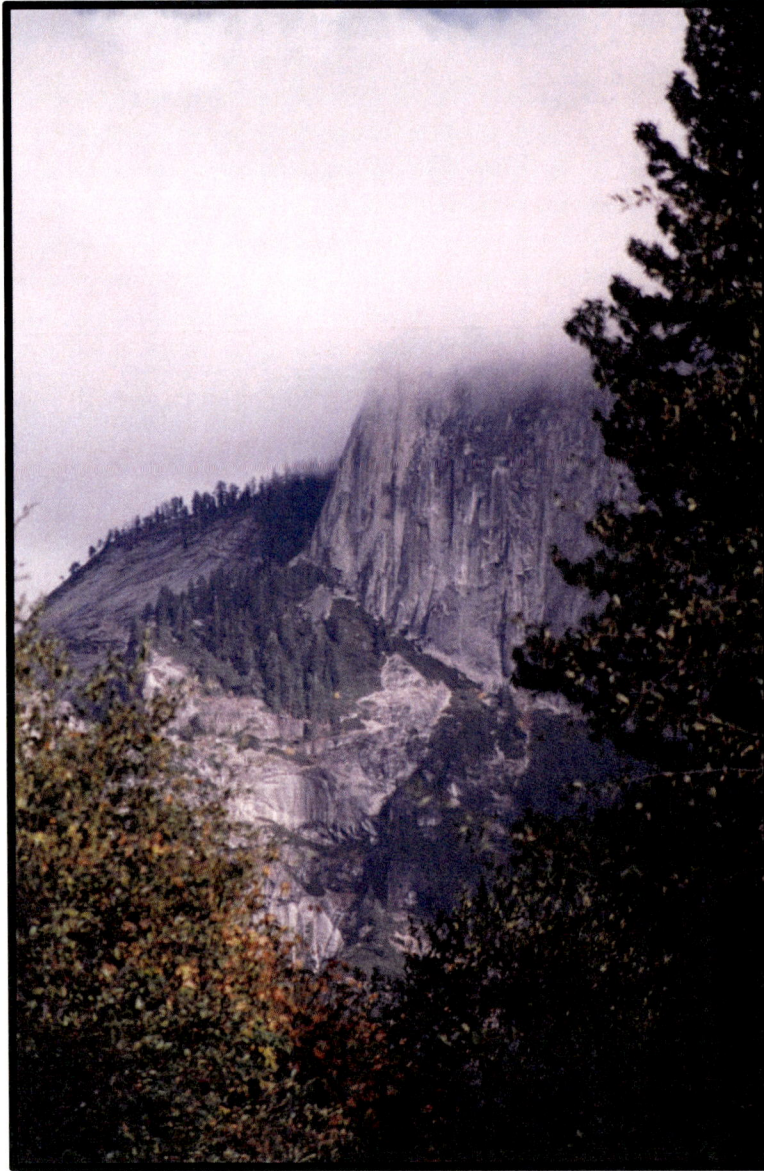

And

scattered

them

over

the land.

Above –

on the mountains,

Below –

in the fields,

— — — — — — — — —

and then –

Chagrin made known his demands.

# "Have no fear! Persevere!

Keep your thoughts and your deeds pure and true.

If you strive to give beauty to others,

The beauty will come back to you!"

Again, to the skies Chagrin raised his voice,

And the heavens answered his call.

47

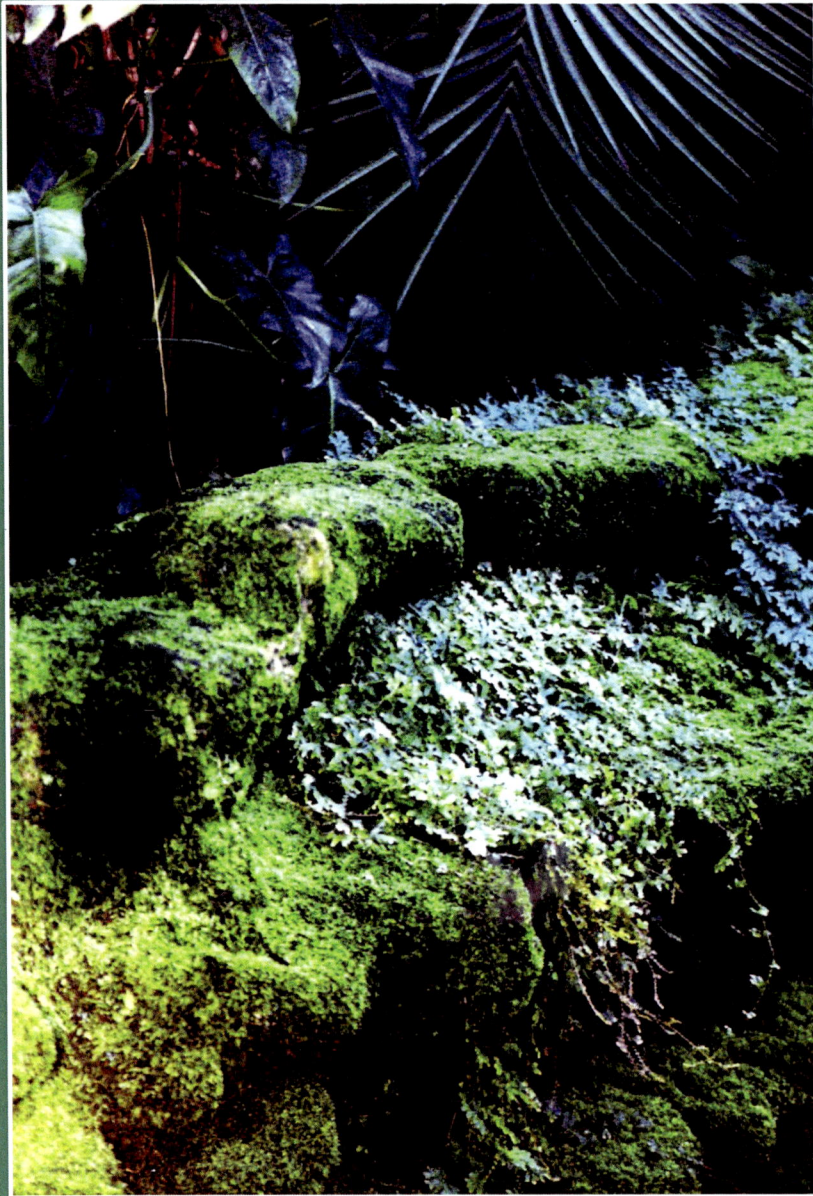

The ground sprouted Pearls of Wisdom...

as the Rain of Rebirth began to fall.

*Happiness*

filled every corner..

The air was alive ...

with *Romance!*

The clouds swept the sky – leaving sunshine.
That's when Chagrin took this stance.

"In your journey through life –
Hold your head high.
Be alert to your friends – and your foes."

Stick to your path —

be true to yourself...

For where the road leads,

*freedom follows ....*

54

"Know this!" said Chagrin with conviction.

"If you strive to work toward your goal,

and nurture your strengths…

(or what you perceive them to be)

*…compassion will maintain your soul."*

# Catalog of Images

# Artist's Statement

## Someone once asked me if I was eclectic.

*-eclectic: adj. 1. (in art, philosophy, etc.) selecting what seems best from various styles, doctrines, ideas, methods, etc. 2. composed of elements drawn from a variety of sources, styles, etc. n. a person who favours an eclectic approach, esp in art or philosophy....*

***That's Me! That's what I am.*** I love art - all kinds. The realistic artists of the Romantic Era have always been my favorites.  I will always be in awe of the works of Michelangelo and Leonardo DaVinci. But, somewhere between childhood and adolescence, I discovered Surrealism and fantasy art, artists like MC Escher and Frank Frazetta added a new dimension to my creative voice. As I have grown, my artwork has evolved. Though, through the years, the need to express myself with images has remained a constant. I am a mixed media artist, and I think a good description of my creative style could be "realistic surrealism".

*It's the simple things in life that inspire me. I was born and raised in rural Wisconsin. That's where I get my love of nature. My artwork comes from the awe I feel when I look at a beautiful sunset, or the feeling of serenity that comes over me when I'm standing near the water. - The world can be a beautiful place if you only take the time to look. -*

Photos of artist; courtesy of jimyoungsphotography

pattyhallart@gmail.com

www.jimyoungs.com

62

This Book is self-published...

Please go to;

www.pattyhallart.com

and click on the link to order;

or

explore my website to view more of my artwork

You can also order this book through;

https://www.createspace.com/3958372

&

www.Amazon.com

Made in the USA
San Bernardino, CA
17 March 2016